W9-AOX-689

Tim Tebow

By Jeff Savage

AMAZING
ATHLETES

Lerner Publications Company • Minneapolis

For Nate Chavez—among the finest athletes in El Dorado Hills

Lerner Publications Company
A division of Lerner Publishing Group, Inc.
241 First Avenue North
Minneapolis, MN 55401 U.S.A.

Website address: www.lernerbooks.com

Library of Congress Cataloging-in-Publication Data

Savage, Jeff, 1961–
    Tim Tebow / by Jeff Savage.
        p.   cm. — (Amazing athletes)
    Includes index.
    ISBN: 978–1–4677–0333–8 (lib. bdg. : alk. paper)
    1. Tebow, Tim, 1987– 2. Football players—United States—Biography 3. Quarterbacks (Football)—
United States—Biography. I. Title.
    GV939.T423S38 2013
    796.332092—dc23 [B]   2012002261

Manufactured in the United States of America
1 – BP – 7/31/12

Table of Contents

Fans filled the seats at Sports Authority Field at Mile High in Denver, Colorado.

TEBOW TIME

Denver Broncos **quarterback** Tim Tebow dropped back to pass. **Defenders** swarmed around him. Tim threw deep down the right side of the field. **Wide receiver** Eddie Royal caught the pass in the **end zone** for a touchdown.

Tim and his team were playing the Pittsburgh Steelers in this 2012 **playoff** game. Tim was the left-handed quarterback who everyone was talking about. He wasn't like most quarterbacks in the National Football League (NFL). Tim ran the ball better than he threw it. His throws were sometimes wildly off. The Steelers had the top-ranked defense in the NFL. Few people gave the Broncos a chance to win.

Tim throws a pass against the Steelers.

Tim is good at running with the football.

The Broncos got the ball back, leading 7–6. Tim completed another deep pass to Demaryius Thomas for 58 yards. Two plays later, Tim ran up the middle for eight yards and another touchdown. Denver led, 14–6.

Over 75,000 fans filled Sports Authority Field at Mile High in Denver. Millions more watched on television. Tim is one of the most liked players in the NFL. He is polite and positive with a strong will to win. This made him popular. Some people were calling Tim the most popular athlete in any sport in the United States.

Tim often prays on the field during games by kneeling and putting his fist on his forehead. Fans started calling this pose Tebowing. People around the world have been photographed while Tebowing.

The Broncos scored two **field goals** to take a 20–6 lead at halftime. The Steelers fought back in the second half. With Denver ahead by seven points, Pittsburgh quarterback Ben Roethlisberger threw a touchdown pass to tie the score, 23–23. The game went to overtime.

Broncos fans cheer after the home team beat the Steelers.

Tim had set a record in 2011 for most comeback wins in a season. Fans started calling the time near the end of a game Tebow Time. Sure enough, on the first play, Tim fired a pass over the middle. Demaryius Thomas caught the ball. Thomas shoved past **cornerback** Ike Taylor and outraced **safety** Ryan Mundy to the end zone. It was an 80-yard touchdown! Broncos fans jumped to their feet and cheered!

Tim's touchdown pass marked the quickest ending to an overtime game in NFL history. Tim crouched on one knee for a moment and put his fist to his forehead. Then he jumped into the stands. "First time I've done that," he said. The winning throw to Thomas was Tim's longest pass as a pro. "I'm very thankful we were able to get the win," Tim said.

Tim celebrates his team's win after the game.

Tim was born in Makati City, Philippines.

HOMESCHOOLED

Timothy Richard Tebow was born August 14, 1987, in the Philippines. Tim's father, Bob, is a pastor who helped run churches in the Southeast Asian country. Tim's mother, Pam, is the daughter of a U.S. Army colonel. Together Tim's parents also ran an **orphanage**. Tim is the youngest of five children. His sisters are Christy and Katie. His brothers are Robby and Peter.

Tim was three years old when his family moved to a 44-acre farm near Jacksonville, Florida. Tim had many chores on the farm. All five children were taught at home by their mother. They studied school subjects and the Bible. The family returned every summer to the Philippines to work at the orphanage.

Tim was good at sports. But at the age of five, he remembers his T-ball coach telling the players that winning did not matter. Tim wondered why not. He wanted to win.

Tim collected sports trading cards. His favorite card was Dallas Cowboys **running back** Emmitt Smith. Smith helped the Cowboys win the Super Bowl three times.

When Tim was nine, he watched the University of Florida Gators win the national title. Tim's parents had met while attending that university.

Tim *(right)* with his mother,
Pam *(left)*, and father, Bob

Children who were taught at home in Florida were allowed to play on local school sports teams. In 2002 when Tim was 15 years old, he played quarterback at Trinity Christian Academy in Jacksonville. His brothers had played **linebacker** at Trinity. But the team did not pass much. Tim wanted to throw the ball more often.

In 2003, Tim transferred to Nease High School in Ponte Vedra, Florida. The Nease High Panthers were a passing team.

By 2004, Tim's strength made him hard to stop on a football field. He could **bench press** 185 pounds 38 times. He set state records for total passing and rushing yards. In 2005, he led Nease High to the state title. In the championship game, the Panthers were protecting a seven-point lead against Armwood High. Tim begged coach Craig Howard to let him play as a defender. Tim and the Panthers stopped Armwood and won the title.

After four seasons of high school football, Tim was ready to move to the next level. More than 80 colleges recruited him. He chose the University of Florida.

Tim didn't play much as a freshman at Florida. He worked hard to become a better football player.

RECORD SETTER

Tim impressed his new Florida Gators teammates. He could throw the ball 70 yards. He could run the 40-yard dash in 4.5 seconds—almost as fast as a track star. He was just a freshman, but he was as strong as many seniors. Strength coach Mickey Marotti had to keep Tim from lifting too much weight. Teammates called Tim the "walking freight truck."

As a freshman in 2006, Tim played backup quarterback behind starter Chris Leak. Tim still finished second on the team in rushing. The Gators won the national title.

Tim became the team's starting quarterback in 2007. In a game against Florida State University, Tim suffered a broken hand. He stayed in the game and threw or ran for five touchdowns. The Gators crushed Florida State, 45–12. Tim played in the Capital One Bowl game wearing a cast on his hand. The Gators lost to the Michigan Wolverines, 41–35.

After the season, Tim was awarded the Heisman Trophy, which is given each year to the most outstanding college football player in the country. Tim became the first sophomore ever to win the award.

Tim holds the Heisman Trophy.

Tim spoke openly about his Christian faith. His teammates were used to it. "He's just a regular guy," said wide receiver Percy Harvin. Millions of people admired Tim. In the six months after the 2007 season, the Gators received over 1,000 requests for Tim to speak. "It can start wearing on you," he said. "But I'm making a lot of people happy by doing this, and that gives me joy."

Quarterbacks feel pressure when the game is on the line. Tim loves this feeling. "That's the best part of being a quarterback," he said. "That's why I've wanted to be a quarterback since I was six years old."

In Tim's junior year, he ran for his 37th career touchdown. The score broke the Gators' record held by Tim's childhood hero, Emmitt Smith. Tim led the Gators to another national championship. Florida beat the University of Oklahoma in the title game, 24–14.

In 2009, Tim suffered a head injury against the University of Kentucky. He spent the night at a hospital. Tim recovered to play the rest of the season. In the Sugar Bowl, Tim set a record with 533 yards passing and running and four touchdowns. The Gators beat the University of Cincinnati, 51–24.

During his time as a member of the Florida Gators, Tim became one of the most successful college quarterbacks ever. It was time for him to move on again.

Tim is hard to tackle when he runs with the ball.

Tim holds his new Broncos jersey after being chosen by the team in 2010.

LEARNING THE GAME

Most football experts thought Tim's style would not work well in the NFL. He often ran with the ball and could get hurt. But the Denver Broncos picked Tim in the first round of the **draft**. Denver fans were excited to have Tim on the team. Before he had even played a game, Tim led all NFL players in jersey sales.

Tim knew he had a lot to learn about the NFL. "I'm very young," he said before the start of the season. "I've got a lot to work on. I know I'll get it."

The 2010 season began with Tim on the bench. He watched starter Kyle Orton. "Every snap when Orton's out there, I'm just trying to play the game in my head," the **rookie** said. In Denver's first 13 games, Tim threw just one pass. Fans in Denver begged the team to put Tim in games.

Many Denver fans wanted Tim to be the team's starting quarterback.

The team did not play well in 2010. Tim got to start the final three games of the season. He led the team to one win, 24–23, over the Houston Texans.

In the fifth game of the 2011 season, Denver trailed the San Diego Chargers at halftime, 23–10. New Broncos head coach John Fox called for Tim. In the fourth quarter, Tim ran for a touchdown and threw for another. The Broncos barely lost, 29–24. Tim walked off the field with fans chanting "Tebow! Tebow!" They wanted him to be the starting quarterback.

Every week during the season, Tim helps someone who is sick or dying. He pays for the person and his or her family to fly to the football game and sit in the stands. He meets with that person on the field before and after the game.

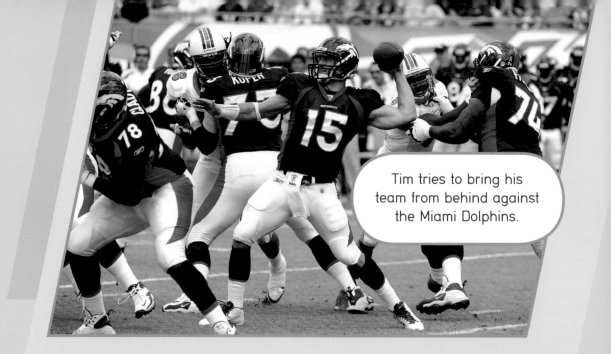

Tim tries to bring his team from behind against the Miami Dolphins.

TEBOWMANIA

The Broncos had a 1–4 record. The 2011 season appeared lost. Denver cut Orton from the team. They named Tim the starting quarterback.

In Tim's first game as the starter, the Broncos trailed the Miami Dolphins, 15–0. Just 2:44 was left in the game. No team in NFL history had ever come back to win a game when behind by so many points with so little time left.

Tim threw a five-yard touchdown pass to Demaryius Thomas. The Broncos got the ball back, trailing 15–7. With 17 seconds left, Tim threw a touchdown pass to Daniel Fells. Tim tied the game by running in a **two-point conversion**. Teammate Matt Prater kicked a field goal in overtime to win it, 18–15.

Tim and teammate Daniel Fells celebrate the two-point conversion.

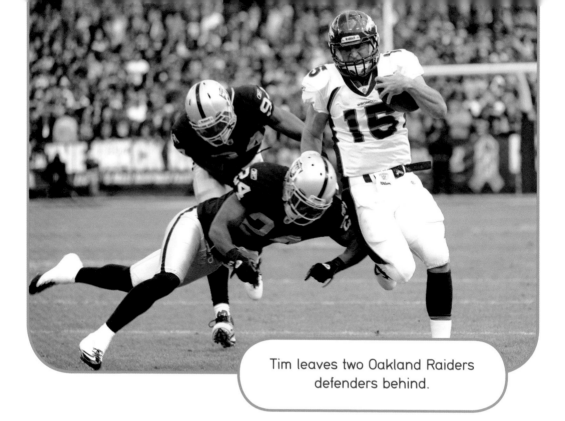

Tim leaves two Oakland Raiders defenders behind.

"You can't lose confidence in yourself, or you've lost already," Tim said after the game. "When you get knocked down, you've got to keep getting back up." In Denver's ninth game of the year, against the Oakland Raiders, Tim rushed for 117 yards. He became just the second quarterback in team history to run for over 100 yards in a game. The Broncos beat the Raiders, 38–24.

Two weeks later, the Broncos trailed the New York Jets by four points late in the game. Tim took the ball at the Jets' 20-yard line. He ran left, then sprinted past defenders and into the end zone with 58 seconds left. The Broncos won, 17–13. After this game, fans began calling the last few minutes of Broncos games Tebow Time.

Denver fans were excited about their new quarterback.

Tim became one of the most popular athletes in the country soon after joining the NFL. He was so popular that his fans were said to have Tebowmania.

The Broncos won their next two games for a record of 8–5. But they lost their final three games. They barely got into the playoffs. Some people wondered if Tim's magic was gone. The answer came in the first round of the playoffs when Tim led the Broncos to a shocking overtime win against the Steelers. Denver's season ended one week later with a loss to Tom Brady and the New England Patriots.

Tim and the Broncos surprised many people with their good play in 2011. But Denver decided to go in a new direction for the 2012 season. They brought in star quarterback Peyton Manning to lead the team. Tim was traded to the New York Jets.

Tim always has time for his fans.

Tim's move to New York made huge news around the country. By this time, he was one of the biggest stars in the NFL. Everyone wanted to know what the move to New York would mean for Tim's future. But as always, Tim took the change in stride. "I'm just having fun with it," he said.

Tim kneels to pray before a game.

Tim wants to keep improving in his new home. "I make a ton of mistakes. But I always get back up and try again," he says. Tim knows he will succeed in the NFL. He takes his own advice when he says, "If you believe, unbelievable things can sometimes be possible. Set your sights high, the higher the better."

Selected Career Highlights

2011 Had most rushing attempts in a game (22)
by a quarterback in at least 50 years
Broke NFL record for most fourth-quarter
comeback wins (6) by a quarterback in
his first 11 starts
Led Broncos to the largest comeback win
(15-point deficit) with less than three minutes
to play in NFL history
Made the longest touchdown run (20 yards) by a
quarterback in the fourth quarter to win a game in
NFL history

2010 Made longest touchdown run by a quarterback (40 yards) in
Broncos history
Became the first quarterback in NFL history to rush for a touchdown
in his first three career starts
Named NFL Rookie of the Week twice

2009 Finished fifth in Heisman Trophy voting
Named *Sports Illustrated* College Football Player of the Decade
Led Gators to a Sugar Bowl win

2008 Led Florida to the BCS national championship
Finished third in Heisman Trophy voting
Won the Maxwell Award as college football player of the year
Broke the Florida career record for rushing touchdowns

2007 Won Heisman Trophy as most outstanding college football player
Named Associated Press Player of the Year
Won Maxwell Award as college football player of the year
Won Davey O'Brien Award as top college quarterback
Set the Southeastern Conference record for most touchdowns in a
season (55)

2006 Helped lead Florida to a national championship
Finished second on the team in yards rushing

2005 Named Florida's Mr. Football
Named First-Team All-State
Named Parade All-American

2004 Named Florida's Mr. Football
Named First-Team All-State

Glossary

bench press: an exercise in which a person lies on a bench with feet on the floor and lifts a weight with both arms

cornerback: a defender who guards the wide receiver

defenders: players whose job is to stop the other team from scoring points

draft: a yearly event in which professional teams take turns choosing new players from a selected group

end zone: the area beyond the goal line at each end of the field. A team scores six points when it reaches the other team's end zone.

field goals: successful kicks over the crossbar and between the two upright poles at each end of the football field. Field goals are worth three points.

linebacker: a defender who guards against both the run and the pass

orphanage: a home where children without parents live

playoff: one game of a series of games held every year to decide a champion

quarterback: in football, the person who throws or hands off the ball

rookie: a first-year player

running back: a football player whose main job is to run with the ball

safety: a defender who plays deep to guard against passes and stop long runs

two-point conversion: a scoring play made immediately after a touchdown that is worth two points. A team can get the two points by running or passing the ball into the opponent's end zone on one play starting from the opponent's two-yard line.

wide receiver: a football player whose main job is to catch passes

Further Reading & Websites

Kennedy, Mike, and Mark Stewart. *Touchdown: The Power and Precision of Football's Perfect Play*. Minneapolis: Millbrook Press, 2010.

Savage, Jeff. *Aaron Rodgers*. Minneapolis: Lerner Publications Company, 2012.

Savage, Jeff. *Mark Sanchez*. Minneapolis: Lerner Publications Company, 2012.

Savage, Jeff. *Tom Brady*. Minneapolis: Lerner Publications Company, 2009.

Denver Broncos: The Official Site
http://www.nfl.com/broncos
The official website of the Denver Broncos that includes the team schedule and game results, late-breaking news, team history, biographies of players like Tim Tebow, and much more.

The Official Site of the National Football League
http://www.nfl.com
The NFL's official website provides fans with the latest scores, schedules, and standings, biographies and statistics of players, as well as the league's official online store.

Sports Illustrated Kids
http://www.sikids.com
The *Sports Illustrated Kids* website covers all sports, including the NFL.

University of Florida: The Official Football Site
http://www.gatorzone.com
The official site of the University of Florida football program that features game results, biographies of current and former players like Tim Tebow, all-time records, the upcoming schedule, and more.

Index

Photo Acknowledgments

The images in this book are used with the permission of: © Jeff Gross/Getty Images, pp. 4, 5, 29; © Ron Chenoy/US Presswire, p. 6; © Chris Humphreys/US Presswire, p. 8; Gary C. Caskey/UPI/Newscom, p. 9; © purpleflames/Flickr/Getty Images, p. 10; © Al Messerschmidt/Getty Images, p. 12; © J. Meric/Getty Images, p. 14; © Kelly Kline/Getty Images, p. 16; © Doug Pensinger/Getty Images, p. 18; AP Photo/Ed Andrieski, pp. 19, 27; Rick Wilking/REUTERS/Newscom, p. 20; © Scott Cunningham/Getty Images, p. 22; © Joe Rimkus Jr./Miami Herald/MCT via Getty Images, p. 23; © Thearon W. Henderson/Getty Images, p. 24; Kellen Micah/ICON SMI/Newscom, p. 25; Rich Gabrielson/ICON SMI/Newscom, p. 28.

Front cover: © Nancy Kaszerman/ZUMA Press/CORBIS.

Main body text set in Caecilia LT Std 55 Roman 16/28.
Typeface provided by Adobe Systems.